I. Introduction

The creation of physician networks has been an important part of the managed care revolution. A network is a panel of physicians whose members have contracted with a third party payer to provide care for enrollees in the payer's health plan.[1] Networks have significant, pro-competitive impacts on health care markets. Scale economies and accumulated expertise on the part of the network results in more efficient search relative to that of individual patients, whose incentives to search for low cost providers may also be dulled by insurance. Networks also enter into "selective contracts" with physicians who, in exchange for higher patient volume, agree to reduced prices and other terms relating to cost control, such as utilization review and capitation. Patient volume is shifted by limiting the physician panel for which enrollees receive full coverage.

Many networks are controlled by payers or independent entrepreneurs or "brokers."[2] Others are controlled by competing physicians, and these can raise serious antitrust concerns. Although there may be gains from improved search and selective contracting in physician-controlled networks, physicians also have incentives to resist changes that reduce their income. Physicians may be able to increase their incomes if they are jointly able to exercise market power through their networks. Network-related agreements might also spill over to reduce competition among physicians for patients outside of network contracts.

_____

[1] We define the term "payers" as all third parties that directly pay providers for some or all of a patient's care. In addition to commercial and public insurers, payers include employers who provide health care benefits as part of employee compensation.

[2] Broker-controlled networks typically charge an access fee to payers who reimburse physicians according to some negotiated fee schedule. Payers also sometimes provide access to their networks to other payers for a fee.

While the anticompetitive dangers of physician-controlled networks are clear, there has been little theoretical or empirical work on why physician control might be efficient relative to other control alternatives. This paper offers a theory explaining why physician-control might be efficient. In Section II we begin our analysis by defining "integration" and "control" in the context of physician networks. Section III presents a theory involving asset specificities in which there can be efficiency gains from physician control. Section IV discusses some of the implications of this analysis for antitrust enforcement.

II. Integration, Control and Physician Networks: Definitions

An understanding of what a physician network is and what "control" and "integration" mean are necessary to appreciate the possible efficiencies from physician control. The concept of integration also has special antitrust significance. The law relies on some determination of integration to distinguish horizontal agreements that might be quickly condemned as *per se* illegal from those agreements, which having passed the integration test, would be subject to a more expansive rule of reason evaluation. However, antitrust law reflects an incomplete understanding of what integration means from an economic perspective.[3] Relying on transactions cost theory, we offer a more complete explanation of what constitutes integration.

We follow Grossman and Hart's approach to defining the firm.[4] They define the firm as being composed of the assets which it owns. Ownership is equivalent to the possession of

---

[3] Although the law typically does not explicitly define "integration," the concept is generally associated with the pooling of resources and the sharing of risks. See ABA Section on Antitrust Law, ANTITRUST LAW DEVELOPMENTS (4th ed. 1997), Vol. 1, pp. 396-8.

[4] Grossman and Hart, *The Costs and Benefits of Ownership: A Theory of Vertical and Lateral Integration*, 94 JOURNAL OF POLITICAL ECONOMY 691 (1986).

the residual rights over assets or actions. Residual rights are those rights not taken away by contract with other parties; rights contractually memorialized are referred to as specific rights. Residual rights exist since it is costly to set down in a contract all possible specific rights. Ownership is the purchase of residual rights of control. The possessed residual rights delimit the boundaries of the firm: that is, the assets, decisions or activities over which the firm is said to be integrated.

While it may also own various physical assets, the most important assets that define a network as a firm are informational intangibles related to the certification of physician panels whose members have particular qualities and who are willing to provide medical services under some set of specified terms. For there to be incentives to create and maintain a network, a network owner must have some residual rights to determine 1) the composition of the physician panel and 2) payer access to it. Determining the panel involves decisions about the number and specialty of physicians to be included.[5] The network is also likely to establish selection criteria based on physician quality,[6] or based on physician willingness to supply

---

[5] The size of the network is a function of the expected number of plan enrollees covered under managed care contracts. Patient accessibility is important to prospective payers, and as a result, the geographic dispersion of panel physicians is another important consideration in assembling a network. If a network is to provide all physician services (rather than just one medical specialty), it must also arrange for an appropriate mix of primary care physicians and specialists.

[6] Networks use various qualitative screens in deciding which physicians to contract with. Nearly all networks review physicians' medical credentials, hospital affiliations and check for adverse malpractice judgments or substance abuse violations. Somewhat less frequently, network evaluators will inspect a physician's office and patient records. The quality of patient record keeping may reveal a great deal about a physician's style of practice. Poorly kept records suggest that a physician is not very careful or well organized. Networks will sometimes also consider quantitative evidence regarding a physician's practice style. For example, a network owned by an insurer that also offers non-managed care insurance products may have access to data on a physician's past claims activity. Networks periodically reassess their panels, and may terminate, or "deselect," certain

(continued...)

services under specified, contractual terms.[7]   Determination of access involves the marketing

of the network to payers and the setting of appropriate access charges.[8]

The degree to which a physician network is integrated depends on its contracts with

physicians, payers and other parties.[9] The are innumerable ways in which the control rights

might be allocated between networks, physicians, payers or other entities with whom a

network might contract.   For example, contractually specifying all the ways in which

utilization review or quality assurance practice protocols might be interpreted or redefined

under all contingencies is obviously very costly.   Contracts between a network and a

---

(...continued)
physicians. In addition to reviewing credentials and malpractice histories, networks use (in varying degrees) consumer complaints, quality review, patient satisfaction surveys and physician "profiling," in determining which physicians should be retained. Physician profiling involves comparing medical outcomes or resource utilization associated with a particular physician with average rates across many physicians. Quality review may focus on physician performance with respect to patient outcomes in specified medical conditions. While deselection may occur because a physician's performance does not meet the network's criteria, a network may deselect physicians if there is a drop in demand or smaller than anticipated growth in patient enrollment. Deselection may also reflect strategic decisions by the network to geographically focus on certain regions or to induce greater volume discounts from remaining panel members.

[7] For example, a network might decide to create a panel of physicians who agree not to contract with other networks or who agree to supply services at some specified discount from their normal charges.

[8] Typically access terms and charges for other services are included in a "master contract" between the network and the payer. Separate "participating physician" agreements between the network and physicians spell out the reimbursement terms for physician services covered by the payer. In addition to price terms, physician agreements include other terms involving practice style and managed care protocols, administrative procedures for billing and reimbursement, and the apportionment of malpractice liability.

[9] Other parties include independent vendors offering various related services such as claims processing, utilization review and actuarial analyses. Networks may contract with such vendors or undertake these functions internally. In some instances, payers contract for these services independently of the network or undertake them in-house. A network also might purchase or rent from other parties various physical assets such as office or diagnostic equipment.

participating physician may state something to the effect that the physician shall follow any practice protocols reasonably established and interpreted by the network. Since the network has some discretion in defining and interpreting the protocols *ex post*, the network has some residual rights regarding the clinical practice of medicine. The network's residual rights in this area would be less if, for example, physician contracts specified that the protocols be tied to local medical standards or some other objective criteria, or if they gave physicians the right to approve any protocol changes. On the other hand, the network generally may have fewer residual rights regarding clinical practice than a group practice with salaried physicians. In the latter case, physician employment contracts are likely to allocate more extensive residual rights in clinical practice to the group practice. The group practice is also likely to have more extensive residual rights to market the services of its physicians as well as greater control of other assets, such as patient records.

In short, a network is more integrated the greater its residual rights over assets or decisions related to the production, marketing and administration of physician services.[10] A network may also have some rights to determine variables relating to competition among panel physicians. Examples here would include physician compensation terms and conditions which affect panel physicians' ability to contract outside of the network. Rights to control these variables should be viewed as another aspect of integration.

---

[10] Similarly, the more physical assets related to the practice of medicine or its administration, such as diagnostic machinery and office equipment, held by the network, the more integrated it is. In this sense, two physicians who practice in the same office, but do not hold any assets in common, may be less integrated than some of the more innovative new forms of collective medical practice, such as clinics without walls, in which many of the assets relating to the practice and administration of medicine are held in common by the network owner, even though the physicians themselves may be in disparate locations.

Since residual rights may be allocated in any number of ways, "control" of a network is a matter of degree. We may define a payer-controlled network as one where residual rights largely belong to either an insurer or employer. Residual rights largely belong to an independent entrepreneur in the broker network case. In a physician-controlled network, the rights are largely held by a significant percentage of the physicians who are members of the network's panel. A physician-controlled network is similar to an employee-owned firm in that a large percentage of the individuals that own the firm work for it under separate contract and that firm ownership is widely shared among the employees.[11] A physician-controlled network becomes a horizontal combination in the antitrust sense when at least some of the controlling physicians are competitors.

III. An Efficiency Theory of Physician-Controlled Networks

It has been argued that large physician group practices or independent practice associations (IPAs) have advantages over individual physicians or small physician groups in contracting with health plans due to economies of scale in administrative functions (in part related to the need for costly information systems) or risk bearing (actuarial advantages due to the law of large numbers).[12] Yet these scale economies are technically achievable whether a network is payer or broker-controlled. The relevant question is whether there are efficiency consequences of who controls the network and this must involve something more than administrative or risk-bearing scale economies.

---

[11] See Russell, *Employee Ownership and Internal Governance*, 6 JOURNAL OF ECONOMIC BEHAVIOR AND ORGANIZATION 217 (1985).

[12] Robinson & Casalino, *Vertical Integration and Organizational Networks in Health Care*, 15 HEALTH AFFAIRS 7 (1996).

This something more is asset specificity in the face of contractual incompleteness. The arms-length trading of the simple competitive model performs well when a buyer can easily turn to any one of a number of competing sellers and when a seller can shift supply from one buyer to another without significant cost. However, when there are transaction-specific assets, parties to an exchange may become locked into a bilateral relationship since these assets cannot be deployed outside the exchange without a loss of value. If contracts are incomplete, the parties may become vulnerable to opportunistic behavior by their trading partner. The threat of opportunism chills investment in transaction specific assets. Various protective safeguards against *ex post* opportunism may be adopted by exchanging parties. These safeguards include contractual provisions to align the incentives of the parties *ex ante* and the creation of a governance structure to maintain harmonious relations *ex post*. These governance structures include informal agreements, detailed explicit contracts and displacing bilateral negotiation through common ownership.[13] The choice among alternative governance structures will depend on their relative costs of implementation and the benefits to the exchanging parties in encouraging transaction-specific investments.

Physician control will be transactionally efficient if 1) physician network-specific investments are significant, 2) network-physician contracts are incomplete and 3) other mechanisms, short of physician control, are not very good substitutes in reducing the threat of opportunism. To simplify the discussion, we assume two organizational control alternatives:

---

[13] For a general review of the relevant literature, see Williamson, *Transaction Cost Economics*, HANDBOOK OF INDUSTRIAL ORGANIZATION (Schmalensee & Willig, eds., 1989). For seminal works see Klein, Crawford & Alchian, *Vertical Integration, Appropriable Rents, and the Competitive Contracting Process*, 21 JOURNAL OF LAW AND ECONOMICS 297 (1978) and Williamson, *Transaction-Cost Economics: The Governance of Contractual Relations*, 22 JOURNAL OF LAW AND ECONOMICS 233 (1979).

a payer-controlled network in which the payer contracts with many individual physicians or small physician groups, and a physician-controlled network comprised of a joint venture among many individual physicians or small physician groups that contract jointly with one or more payers.[14] We further assume that payers have insurance contracts with employers who provide health insurance benefits for their employees.

A. Physician Reputational Investments. We assume physicians seek to maximize the value of their practices and in large part this involves building a solid patient base. Efforts to build a patient base can be regarded as investments in reputation.[15] In a world of selective contracting, efforts to be admitted and to be retained on network panels are important in this regard. Once admitted to a network, physicians expend further effort in securing a patient base as they compete with other panel physicians for patients covered under employer contracts. Some of these reputational efforts are directed toward building personal

---

[14] We ignore the broker-controlled network alternative as well as the alternatives in which payers integrate into medical services by employing large panels of physicians and other health care providers (Kaiser Permanente is perhaps the classic example of this kind of "network"). Many physician networks are hybrids. For example, some payers assemble networks by both contracting with individual physicians and with others who are members of a physician-controlled IPA or who are members of large multi-speciality group practices. While it is beyond the scope of this paper to do, a comprehensive treatment of the reorganization of the physician services industry in response to managed care would need to assess the relative benefits of these alternatives as well as related issues, such as the significance of physician-hospital organizations (PHOs) and management service organizations (MSOs), entities which appear largely motivated by managed care initiatives.

[15] Reputation is an important component of the value of a physician's practice and, as an accounting matter, is that part of a practice's value attributable to goodwill. According to one survey of practice valuations between 1985 and 1995, the median value of goodwill is somewhere between 25 and 30 percent of annual gross revenues for many physician specialities. However, in some suburban and metropolitan practices, goodwill value may be as high as 75% of annual gross revenues. It also appears that in areas like California, where managed care is particularly advanced, traditional goodwill valuations have been replaced by per covered life valuations based on a practices's managed care contracts. See Rose, *Selling a practice? Good will may boost your take*, MEDICAL ECONOMICS, (September 25, 1995) at 14.

relationships with patients.[16] Other efforts are aimed at other physicians, particularly those with whom referral relationships might be established.[17]

Reputational investments made by physicians upon joining a network would appear to result in significant asset specificities.[18] These reputational investments are transaction-specific to the extent they cannot be fully redeployed outside the network. Redeployability largely depends on how easily a physician can get network patients to switch to other networks to which the physician belongs should the physician voluntarily leave or be deselected or should the network lose the insurance contract with an employer. If patients switch networks

---

[16] The importance of reputation in physician services markets has long been recognized in the economic literature. See e.g., Gaynor, *Adam Smith as Health Economist, Redux. Professor Smith on the Market for Physician Services*, 13 JOURNAL OF HEALTH ECONOMICS 119 (1994); and Getzen, *A Brand Name Theory of Medical Group Practice*, 33 JOURNAL OF INDUSTRIAL ECONOMICS 199 (1984). A good reputation attracts patients and increases their loyalty. A new patient may consult with a physician based on the experience of friends, relatives or co-workers. These individuals may or may not have the same health care plan or access the physician through the same network as the new patient. While much of a physician's reputation with a patient (or with referring physicians) derives from the physician's skill and knowledge, other aspects derive from the personal relationships that a physician establishes with his or her patients and the physician's effort in diagnosing and treating a medical problem. Patients often provide information to a physician imprecisely as in a code, and to be effective, the physician must be attentive in interpreting that code and in communicating back to the patient in an understandable and sympathetic manner. The promptness with which calls are returned from a distressed patient, the accommodation of emergency appointments, the physician's regularity in making hospital rounds, the competence and helpfulness of the physician's medical and administrative assistants and the physician's overall diligence in diagnosis and treatment as perceived by the patient are all efforts which contribute to reputation.

[17] A physician's reputation as perceived by other physicians is also an important asset. A physician will receive more referrals if he or she is perceived as a high quality provider. A referring physician also needs to be informed about the quality of receiving physicians: poor referral choices will adversely affect a physician's reputation with patients and may increase the risk of malpractice claims. Physicians slowly establish their reputation with other physicians through hospital medical staff or local medical society interactions, through informal consultations and covering arrangements with colleagues and through feedback from referred patients.

[18] Physicians also own office or diagnostic equipment or other important intangible assets such as human capital from medical school training or hospital admitting privileges. Although there may be exceptions, these assets are not likely to be specific to any network.

to stay with the physician, the reputational investments made with these patients are not network-specific. While much of a physician's reputational capital with other physicians may be fruitfully redeployed, there may also be some loss in a physician's leaving a network since only intra-network referrals are often permitted.

In some cases, the costs to patients in switching networks to stay with their physician will be quite low. For example, patients enrolled in a Medicare HMO program have been able to switch to another Medicare HMO at essentially zero cost at the beginning of each month. If a physician belongs to multiple Medicare HMO networks, opportunism by any one network would be limited since many patients may follow any physician who left or was excluded from the network.

In other cases, some patients will be deterred from following physicians by the increased expenses incurred in changing health plans. Medicare enrollees who have to switch from a Medicare HMO program to the traditional fee-for-service Medicare program to stay with their physician would face large co-pays for both inpatient and outpatient services and would lose insurance coverage of prescription drugs and various other services.[19]

Patients enrolled in private pay managed care programs also may face significant costs in switching plans to stay with their physician. According to one national survey of employer sponsored health insurance, about 23 percent of employees were offered only a PPO or an HMO plan.[20] Unless they were willing to bear the full cost of insurance, these employees

---

[19] These gaps in Medicare coverage may be filled in with the purchase of supplemental "Medigap" insurance.

[20] Bucci & Grant, *Employer-sponsored health insurance: what's offered; what's chosen*, MONTHLY LABOR REVIEW (October 1995) at 42. The study also indicated that for those firms which offered

(continued...)

would not have the option of switching to another insurance plan if their physician were deselected from their plan's network. Another 9 percent of employees were offered both a PPO and HMO option without a fee-for service option. Many of these employees also may not have the option of switching to another network that includes their physician should the physician leave the network. Moreover, even if enrollees have the option of electing a different plan and network which includes the physician, and do not have to incur any additional out-of pocket costs, other considerations, such as a desire to maintain relationships with other physicians or health care providers, may discourage switching.

The extent to which patients might follow their physicians, despite incurring higher costs, will vary across patients and is likely to depend on various factors including patient income and the strength of the existing physician-patient bond. Nonetheless, some evidence suggests that a significant percentage of a physician's patients might not follow if they had to bear significantly higher insurance or out of pocket costs. Significant actual or predicted losses in physician patient loads have also been reported where networks have deselected

---

[20](...continued)
health insurance benefits about 35 percent of employees chose either an PPO or HMO option. Larger firms were more likely than smaller ones to offer choices in health plans.

physicians.[21] Physicians also appear acutely concerned about potential losses in patient bases if a network loses important payer contracts.[22]

Once physicians expend effort in building good relationships with network patients and other network physicians, they are likely to view other networks as less perfect substitutes compared with their evaluations *ex ante*. Physicians conceivably could compensate patients (or other physicians) for moving outside the network. Even if such compensation were feasible, this would be a cost of redeploying physicians' reputational assets outside the network.

B.   Other Network Specific Investments by Physicians. In addition to efforts directed toward individual network patients, physician efforts to promote the network more generally may also be important transaction specific investments. These may involve efforts to achieve the network's overall cost and quality objectives, either by modifying individual practice styles or by cooperating with other panel physicians to improve network performance. Professional or social interactions may play an important role in these regards, and favorable testimonials from current panel members might also facilitate attracting desirable new physicians to a network. These network promotional efforts may be very important since the "brand name"

---

[21] In one reported instance, which appears representative of the potential losses in patient base upon deselection from a PPO network, one physician practice lost half of its network patients within a few months after deselection, even though patients could have continued their relationship with the physician had they been willing to pay between 10 and 20 percent more in out of pocket costs. See Terry, *When Health Plans Don't Want You Anymore*, MEDICAL ECONOMICS, (May 23, 1994) at 123. For additional accounts of the actual or potential impact of deselection upon physician practices see Pretzer, *Deselected Doctors vs. the Blues: Who Really Won?*, MEDICAL ECONOMICS, (October 9, 1995) at 182; and Rice, *Can a Health Plan Deselect You Without Cause?*, MEDICAL ECONOMICS, (February 24, 1997) at 223.

[22] See Hurley, Lake, Gold & Almond, *Arrangements Between Managed Care Plans and Physicians II* (1996) at 74.

of the entire network appears to be playing an increasingly large role in the market for physician services.[23]

C. Contractual Incompleteness and Network Reputation as a Performance Bond. If exchanging parties were able to write and easily enforce a contract which details the parties' rights and obligations under all important future contingencies, transaction-specific investments would not be chilled. A complete physician-network contract would specify the level of physician effort and how the surplus from physician reputational and promotional investments would be apportioned between the network and the physician. Effort and strategic decisions by the network would also have to be taken into account since the return to physicians' effort also depends on these variables.[24] For example, physicians might regard

---

[23] There are other transaction-specific investments but these may not be either very significant in magnitude or their compensation may be relatively easily contractible. Such investments include learning a network's administrative procedures, clinical protocols, and learning or other costs in connecting a physician to a network's information management system. That these investments are not very sensitive to opportunistic risks is suggested by the fact physicians often join multiple networks in spite of such costs.

[24] The value of physician reputational investments are sensitive to changes in a network's strategic plans. If an HMO, for example, decides it does not want to concentrate on a particular region, it might reduce advertising, increase per enrollee prices, or reduce the quality or scope of ancillary services. Physicians in the HMO's network will experience losses to the extent that employer contracts are lost or are renewed on less favorable terms. Alternatively, a network might be very aggressive in signing up new employers, but might not make sufficient increases in the size of its physician panel, resulting in congestion in individual physician offices and forcing physicians to spend less time on average with patients.

A network might also sign new contracts involving enrollees who are less profitable for physicians to treat than those under existing contracts, but require panel physicians to minister to the new group as a condition for continuing participation in other, more profitable network contracts. A possible example is Blue Cross/Blue Shield of Tennessee's requirement that physicians participating in its commercial PPO network also accept patients enrolled in the state's TennCare program for the poor. In 1993, Blue Cross signed a contract with the state to provide care to TennCare enrollees using its Tennessee Preferred Network (TPN) of providers. TPN physicians characterized the arrangement as a "cram down" requirement, and for a while the number of participating physicians in TPN dropped from 6,500 to 3,500. By the end of 1994, however, almost all physicians had returned to the network.
(continued...)

their reputational investments in patients or the network as excessive *ex post* if a network took actions which caused employers not to renew contracts.

Actual physician-network contracts are clearly incomplete. The contracts are typically short term, often one year with automatic renewal options for both parties. This contract duration is significantly shorter than the time horizon over which physicians establish reputations with individual patients and other physicians and benefit from those investments. Even within the stated duration of a contract, a network usually retains rights to alter important terms.[25] For example, networks often reserve a right to change utilization or quality assurance protocols without notice. Contractual language relating to termination is often general or vague about the grounds for termination, and some contracts give the network the right to deselect without notice or cause. Moreover, as we have seen, networks retain residual rights with respect to marketing the network to employers. Instances of networks opportunistically appropriating the surplus from network specific investments by physicians will not be frequently observed if physicians generally anticipate opportunistic behavior. Nonetheless, network specific investments will still be chilled at the margin if contracts are incomplete. This margin is set balancing the gains to the exchanging parties of additional specific investments against the increased costs of writing and enforcing more detailed contracts.

---

[24](...continued)
See Bonnyman, *Stealth Reform: Market Based Medicaid in Tennessee*, 15 HEALTH AFFAIRS 306 (1996).

[25] See Caesar, *How to Gain Leverage with a Health Plan*, MEDICAL ECONOMICS, (February 7, 1994) at 32.

Explicit, legally enforceable contracts are not the only mechanism to achieve efficient exchange where there are asset specificities. Parties often rely on "implicit contracts" wherein the market consequences of lost future business suffered by a party that behaves opportunistically may assure fair dealing and contractual performance. Reputation acts a performance bond. Implicit contracts may be a transactionally cheaper way to encourage transaction specific investments than solely relying on detailed explicit contracts. Establishing reputation is costly however, and this cost (plus any transactions costs of writing and enforcing explicit contracts) will be balanced at the margin against the incremental gain to the exchanging parties from additional transaction specific investments.

Potential reputational losses no doubt limit potential opportunism by non-physician controlled networks.[26] Yet the degree to which reputation can effectively serve as an implicit contract between networks and physicians exists in a continuum. For a network expecting to add physicians to its panel, reputation is more likely to be an effective bonding device since opportunistic behavior may make it very costly for the network to increase panel size. For a network not expecting to grow, reputation may be less likely to deter opportunism since the gain from opportunism is more likely to outweigh the loss from increased difficulties in signing up new physicians in future periods. The effectiveness of implicit contracts also critically depends on how easily opportunistic behavior can be observed and distinguished

---

[26] Gold *et al* report that although managed care networks are under intense competitive pressures to contain costs, "there are important market protections against plan actions to arbitrarily and frequently reconfigure their networks. Plans do not want to develop reputations for treating physicians unfairly or for interfering with established physician-patient relationships." (Gold, Nelson, Lake, Hurley & Berenson, *Behind the Curve: A Critical Assessment of How Little Is Known About Arrangements Between Managed Care Plans and Physicians*, 52 MEDICAL CARE RESEARCH AND REVIEW (1995) at 319.)

from non-opportunistic responses to changes in demand, costs or competitive conditions.[27]

Distinguishing opportunistic behavior may be problematic where demand, cost and competitive

conditions are as unsettled as they are in many health care markets.[28]

     D.   The Gain from Physician Control. There would be a gain from physician control

if any given level of network specific reputational or promotional efforts by panel physicians

could be secured more cheaply (either by reducing the costs of enforcing explicit contracts or

from reducing the cost of establishing a reputation for fair dealing) as compared to relying on

contractual alternatives with little or no physician control. There are several reasons to expect

that reputational and promotional effort might be more easily secured with physician control.

First, the gains of opportunistic behavior at the network level and corresponding losses at the

physician level would be internalized. As a result, a physician-controlled network should be

less likely to take actions that would harm or create losses for its panel members, everything

else equal. Consequently a physician controlled network may have an advantage securing the

trust of physicians, thus economizing on reputational bonding expenses. Second, opportunism

---

[27] For a discussion raising skepticism on reputation's effectiveness in discouraging opportunism on these and other grounds see Williamson, THE MECHANISMS OF GOVERNANCE, 151-158 (1996).

[28] As one managed care expert observed, "(a) plan can try to distinguish itself in its interactions with providers, but it is restrained by the market requirement to compete on the basis of a broad network and low prices. Treating physicians 'better' than the competition, by implementing more doctor-friendly utilization management programs or simply by paying more, is not rewarded if the doctors remain in the plans they dislike....In self-correcting markets, physicians would quit plans that do not pay enough or that interfere with their ability to care for patients. However, quitting a plan causes a disruption in patient care, especially when patients cannot switch plans to keep their physicians. Because of the potential economic loss as well as loyalty to patients, physicians tend not to quit. The result is that plans see no need to stop screwing down on provider reimbursement as their main cost containment technique." See Berenson, *Beyond Competition*, 16 HEALTH AFFAIRS (1997) at 175-6. How much of such reductions in provider reimbursements should be attributed to competitive pressures as opposed to opportunistic behavior is not likely to be clear.

by payers with whom the physicians jointly contract may be reduced due to economies of scale in monitoring and enforcing contracts.[29] There may also be related economies in negotiating contracts with payers which would allow physicians to switch more quickly and easily away from a payer who behaves opportunistically, thereby reducing the gains to opportunism.[30] Third, there may be savings in governing physician-network contracts since fellow physicians are in the best position to solve problems or persuade their peers to adhere to courses of actions consistent with network objectives. Peer pressure may be an effective device for governing the network.[31] According to Robinson and Casalino, physician groups appear better

---

[29] In this limited regard a physician controlled network plays a role similar to that of a union whose members have firm-specific human capital. Union monitoring of contracts may reduce opportunism since it reduces the lag with which opportunistic behavior by an employer is detected. A union also creates employee bargaining power, and this may deter contract violations since an employer could be more easily punished. See Klein, Crawford, and Alchian, *supra* note 13, at 315. Employee bargaining power may exist even though employees do not have market power *ex ante*.

[30] One recent physician survey suggests that these advantages may be particularly significant. The leading reason given for practices joining together either through affiliations in which practices maintained separate identities or through mergers, was to be in a better position to negotiate with health insurers. See Project HOPE Center for Health Affairs, *Results of the Physician Payment Review Commission's 1994 National Survey of Physicians* (1995).

[31] Peer pressure has its basis in the ongoing relationships among physicians, relationships not necessarily confined to a network. Physicians interact in referring and receiving patients from each other, providing back-up coverage, consulting with each other on difficult cases or common business problems, serving on hospital medical staffs and associated staff committees, and by participating in local medical societies. Some of these interactions may be merely social in nature, but may nonetheless be a significant basis for peer pressure. Key to a physician's success in such interaction is the esteem commanded by the physician with his or her peers. Panel physicians that act contrary to the interests of the network run the risk of losing that esteem, thereby possibly jeopardizing other relationships. This aspect of physician peer pressure is supported by transaction costs literature suggesting that if parties to an agreement are involved in a broader trading relationship, continuity of the agreement may be facilitated. See Klein, Crawford and Alchian, *supra* note 13, at 305; Kogut, *The Stability of Joint Ventures: Reciprocity and Competitive Rivalry*, 38 JOURNAL OF INDUSTRIAL ECONOMICS 183 (1989); and Williamson, *Credible Commitments: Using Hostages to Support an Exchange*, 73 AMERICAN ECONOMIC REVIEW 519 (1983).

Non-physician controlled networks attempt to utilize peer pressure in controlling physician

(continued...)

able to manage utilization of member physicians in a cooperative rather than adversarial manner as compared to non-physician controlled networks, which are more likely to be viewed as "third parties" intervening in clinical decision making.[32] Similarly, Hillman, Welch and Pauly conclude that the effectiveness of physician risk pools in controlling costs may depend more strongly on managerial control effected by peer pressure rather than the shifting of financial risk itself.[33]

These considerations suggest that physician control of networks may be efficiency-enhancing relative to non-physician control alternatives. How large this efficiency gain might be is unclear. We suspect any gain is more likely to be significant where relatively sophisticated medical cost control stratagems are attempted, since reliance on detailed explicit or implicit contracts by non-physician controlled networks may be less effective. Possible evidence supporting this proposition is that in California, arguably the state where managed care is most highly evolved, HMOs now typically contract with physician-controlled IPAs or

---

[31](…continued)
behavior as well, such as by having network physicians serve on committees establishing clinical pathways or overseeing utilization review. However, the scope that non-physician controlled networks have for utilizing this device in order to obtain network objectives is far more limited than is the case with physician controlled networks. For example, given the difficulties in contracting over every aspect of a physician's utilization review activities, network physicians are likely to be less persuaded by a doctor whose financial incentives they perceive as different from their own.

[32] See Robinson & Casalino, *The Growth of Medical Groups Paid Through Capitation in California,* 333 THE NEW ENGLAND JOURNAL OF MEDICINE 1684 (1995).

[33] Hillman, Welch & Pauly, *Contractual Arrangements between HMOs and Primary Care Physicians: Three-Tiered HMOs and Risk Pools*, 30 MEDICAL CARE 136 (1992).

large group practices rather than contracting with physicians directly. These physician groups are paid on a capitated basis to provide and manage physician and other medical services.[34]

To illustrate why physician control may especially matter where managed mechanisms are particularly complex consider capitation where physicians are at financial risk for care rendered by other physicians and other health care providers. Under such arrangements there are numerous dimensions which affect physician compensation, including patient demographics, the size of the physician pool, the identity of the physicians within the pool and network incentives or penalties to align physician behavior. While payers can and do set up and manage capitated panels contractually, given all the terms which affect physician compensation and responsibility, and the difficulties inherent in measuring such terms, such contracts are generally very incomplete, and it may be more efficient transactionally to do so if the physicians controlled the network.[35]

Similarly, reliance on explicit or implicit contracts without physician control may not be very effective in eliciting innovation since contractually specifying obligations *ex ante* is likely to be very difficult and detecting and even defining opportunistic behavior may be

---

[34] See Robinson and Casalino, *supra* note 32; see also Physician Payment Review Commission, *Arrangements Between Managed Care Plans and Physicians* (1995), at 195-200.

[35] Another possible area of contractual incompleteness under capitation is that it is often difficult to specify exactly what services are within a particular physicians' scope of practice. Thus, patients may find themselves exposed to clinical risks if a plan refuses a provider request for authorization of specialist services that the provider does not feel competent to provide. The difficulties in describing service duties can also expose the physician to far greater levels of financial liability than he may have expected. Similar clinical and financial risks also exist in fee-for-service managed care arrangements when either prospective and/or retrospective utilization controls are in place. However, under prospective and concurrent utilization review, the risks appear to be more clinical in nature, while under retrospective review the risks would appear to be more financial in nature.

especially hard. If physician cooperation is necessary to exploit important innovation opportunities, physician control may be vastly superior over payer control. This is consistent with Robinson and Casalino's conclusion that innovation relies not only on formal cost reduction and quality improvement mechanisms, but perhaps even more importantly on informal mechanisms that realign provider incentives:

> The early gains from managed care are easy: lower fees for specialists, shorter lengths-of-stay for hospital patients, and fewer high-cost tests for the worried well. But the marketplace pressure to economize persists after all this low-hanging fruit has been picked. The delivery systems that maintain their advantage under managed care have the ability to innovate continually in evaluating their own performance, improving their own quality of care, and controlling their own costs through internal peer review, combining economic efficiency with a culture of professionalism. [36]

Nonetheless, non-physician controlled networks may not be totally displaced in the market even if there are significant gains to physician control. Physicians are likely to be heterogeneous in their preferences for control and in their sensitivity to opportunistic risks. Patient and payer preferences may also be differentiated. Control alternatives may coexist in the market if they offer differing price/quality combinations.

Moreover, integration must be regarded as a continuum, and it may not be efficient to allocate all residual rights from payers to physicians. Physicians may have private incentives to behave opportunistically against payers by either trying to circumvent cost controls or by trying to get patients to switch to other plans. Physician opportunism, everything else equal, would tend to dull incentives of payers to develop and market healthplans. Payers might try to

---

[36] Robinson & Casalino, *supra* note 12, at 13.

impose various contractual restrictions (e.g. exclusivity provisions) on individual physicians or physician groups, but at some point allocating fewer residual rights to physicians creates disincentives for physician effort. As a result, the efficient allocation of residual rights between physicians and payers will reflect a balancing of the opportunistic risks as viewed from both sides of the exchange.[37]

IV. Concluding Remarks: Implications for Antitrust

Antitrust law and its practitioners have not fully understood the economic concept of integration, and as a result the legal view of the possible efficiencies in physician-controlled networks is somewhat off the mark. For example, under the prevailing legal view physician-controlled networks offer potential efficiency benefits if physicians jointly bear medical utilization risks by accepting capitated contracts. Under our theory, the real gain to physician-controlled networks derives not from the presence of risk-bearing itself: instead the real gain is that it may be cheaper transactionally to secure whatever medical resource savings that might be induced by capitation through physician control relative to organizational alternatives where physicians have little or no control.

How large the efficiency gain to physician control is remains unclear. At any rate, our analysis implies that harsh antitrust treatment of physician controlled networks, based on an

---

[37] A 1994 survey of managed care plans that contracted with physician groups found that the groups tended to have primary responsibility for physician selection and payment policy, while the plans were much more likely to retain control over quality assurance and utilization functions. See Hurley, Lake, Gold & Almond, *supra* note 22 at 66-71. We suspect that the allocations of rights between physicians and plans is still in flux with one relatively recent trade press account suggesting that payers are increasingly delegating network creation and particular managed care functions (e.g., utilization review, claims payments, quality improvement programs) to organized physician groups. (Jaklevic, *Take this Job and…this Job…and that Job*, MODERN HEALTHCARE (July 7, 1997) at 36.

observation that networks may be organized without physician control, is not appropriate. Recent revisions in antitrust policy which clarify the circumstances in which physician controlled networks would be judged under a rule of reason rather than a *per se* standard are consistent with a more expansive view of the efficiency potential of physician-controlled networks.[38]

Our efficiency rationale by no means implies that physician-controlled networks pose no competitive problems. Physician-controlled networks can well be cartel devices in which any efficiency gain from integration is swamped by anticompetitive price increases on physician services. Our analysis implies, however, that *per se* rules or truncated rule of reason approaches that do not encompass some examination of market power should be used very sparingly in determining antitrust liability for physician-controlled networks. First, the recognition that residual rights delimit the boundaries of a firm underscores the fact that integration must be regarded as a continuum, reflecting differing allocations of rights between a network, payers, physicians, and other entities, along many dimensions. Accordingly, the search by antitrust enforcers for bright lines to distinguish "integrated" horizontal arrangements from purely anticompetitive cartels may be unproductive.

Transactions cost theory also suggests that antitrust should be careful not to overvalue integration in distinguishing between procompetitive and anticompetitive horizontal arrangements. The optimal allocation of residual rights will reflect a balance of opportunistic

---

[38] See U.S. Department of Justice and Federal Trade Commission, *Statements of Antitrust Enforcement Policy in Health Care,* (1996). Like its predecessors, the most recent version of the Statements retain *per se* treatment for physician-controlled networks which do not sufficiently distinguish themselves from mere price-fixing cartels by undertaking other activities (e.g. quality controls, assumption of insurance risk) that arguably reduce costs or are valuable to buyers.

risks on both sides of an exchange. Consequently, "more" integration by physicians is not

necessarily efficient. Furthermore, agreements otherwise subject to opportunistic behavior

may be stabilized by embedding them in a broader trading relationship. We touched on this

notion above in noting how involvement by network physicians in other physician relationships

may promote cohesion in a pro-competitive network joint venture. Just as with procompetitive

ventures, nearly every anticompetitive cartel also has its opportunists, which in this case are its

potential defectors. The stability of a cartel typically depends on its ability to monitor

adherence and to cajole, coerce and ultimately to impose losses on defectors. Mechanisms to

oversee and coordinate physician activity, or which require physicians to make costly

commitments to their network which they cannot fully recoup upon leaving, may also act to

stabilize an anticompetitive agreement in addition to being related to the network's

procompetitive undertakings.

Second, it is difficult to estimate the efficiency consequences of modifying the

allocation of residual rights, particularly when those consequences involve subtle, long term

effects on the incentives to make transaction-specific investments or the ease with which a

complex transaction might be governed. Our analysis suggests that antitrust challenge of

various joint venture "collateral restraints" on competitively sensitive variables--restraints

which from a transactions cost perspective are just another aspect of integration--may be

inappropriate unless these effects are fully understood. Consider collateral restraints on price.

Suppose a health plan puts together a physician network. To define and market the network,

the plan must make various decisions, including decisions related to prices paid to physicians.

Administrative advantages of having a standardized pricing schedule need to be balanced against the savings or inducement value of having different price schedules for individual physicians. The number of physicians willing to participate in the network is likely to be sensitive to the price level that the network is willing to pay. The network's physician pricing decisions thus have implications for the qualitative nature of the network. Being able to make such decisions represent residual rights enjoyed by the owner of the network. The incentives to develop a network depend on having some residual rights to define and market it. If the panel physicians were to form a joint venture to buy the network from the plan, antitrust enforcers might consider these same decisions as horizontal agreements and might strike them down as not being ancillary to the joint venture. Depriving the physician-controlled network of the ability to make such pricing decisions may well have negative incentive effects with respect to network specific investments at both the physician and network level. The magnitude of these effects will be far from obvious, but almost certainly will be more difficult to assess than whether the physicians have market power.

www.ingramcontent.com/pod-product-compliance
Lightning Source LLC
Chambersburg PA
CBHW081251170526

45165CB00009B/3284